UNTIL CHRIST BE FORMED IN YOU

A REGNUM CHRISTI ESSAY ON OUR APPROACH TO FORMATION IN THE MOVEMENT

FR. DANIEL BRANDENBURG, LC

D1410485

ISBN-10: 1976352517

ISBN-13: 978-1976352515

TABLE OF CONTENTS

FOREWORD

FOREWORD: WHAT ARE RC ESSAYS?

RC Essays are extended, in-depth reflections on particular aspects of life as a Regnum Christi member. An Essay may develop the nature of a virtue, showing what that virtue might look like when lived out in harmony with the Regnum Christi identity and mission. An Essay may explore the challenges of living out one of the commitments shared by all members. An Essay may be instructive, explaining the history, context, and meaning of certain Movement traditions. In short, RC Essays are a chance for all of us to delve deeper into our charism, reflecting seriously on our spiritual patrimony, which the Church has recognized and lauded, and in that way helping that patrimony grow and bear fruit.

RC Essays make no pretense of being the sole and exhaustive expression of our charism. The RC Spirituality Center will review and edit them to ensure their quality in expression and content, but no single person owns a collective charism in such a way as to give it a definitive and exhaustive expression. This is one of the important lessons we have begun to learn in our process of reform and renewal.

Some RC Essays will lend themselves naturally to personal meditation; others will be especially apt for group study circles; all aim to be useful as spiritual reading for members in every branch of the Movement.

It is our hope and prayer that this series will continue to grow organically under the Holy Spirit's guidance. Some Essays will connect more strongly with our members, and others less, while some may fall by the wayside after their useful moment has passed. Yet perhaps the best

RC Essays will stand the test of time, becoming spiritual and intellectual nourishment for many generations of Movement members.

Please send your ideas and feedback to us through the feedback button at RCSpirituality.org.

UNTIL CHRIST BE
FORMED IN YOU

INTRODUCTION

I do not pretend to have any special qualifications to write this essay. I've never been a formator in a seminary, never been a superior in a Legionary community, and certainly was never a "formator" in Regnum Christi before joining the Legion. But I suppose I'm like one of those mountain adventure writers who has never scaled Mount Everest, but has a smidgen of firsthand experience climbing and has observed enough of the successes and failures of others to be able to write a compelling story.

And the story of formation in Regnum Christi is a critical one. After all, none of us is perfect. We all need formation. There's a whole chapter about it in the RC Member Handbook (nn. 385 to 391), and numerous references throughout the entire text, such as these two numbers which give us the proper context for understanding the importance Regnum Christi places on formation:

> 356. In order to be able to offer an effective service to the Church, Regnum Christi knows that it must have well-formed members, motivated and trained to take on the great challenges of the apostolate in today's world. This is an unavoidable demand since nothing can take the place of formation.

> 357. The formation the Movement offers its members seeks to be as well-rounded as possible, addressing their spiritual, intellectual, human, and apostolic preparation. This takes into account the need to prepare the person in all his dimensions so that God can forge him into a true apostle. Formation in Regnum Christi is formation for the mission.

It seems to me that three questions about formation in Regnum Christi have been adequately answered already: we know *why* we seek formation (for the mission), we know *what kind* of formation to seek (integral), and we know *the tools* at our disposition to form ourselves (cf. 388–390 RCMH).

But there is another question that seems less adequately resolved: *how* do you form someone? When you are personally motivated, it's simple enough for you to seek out formation and better yourself. But what do you do when you are in a position to help others, or when you are responsible for your own children or for the formation of students, employees, parish youth, or RC section members? When someone is lacking knowledge, will, drive, experience, passion—or even the desire to attain what they are lacking—how can we move them toward the fullness God wants for them? That *how* isn't so clear.

In the pages that follow, we'll explore this *how* in three chapters: (1) How *not* to form someone, (2) How Jesus formed his disciples, and (3) Implications for Regnum Christi. By the end of this essay, you won't have all the answers, but you'll have a clearer picture about how to form someone.

I. HOW *NOT* TO FORM SOMEONE

If we tried to figure out how to form someone by just alluding to a checklist of dos and don'ts, I think we would miss the point. Formation is more than a process; it's the art of motivating a person to become all that God calls them to be. That's why I begin not with *how*, but with *how not*, since often the best way to see something clearly is to first see what it is *not*.

Over the years, I have been blessed with wonderful and holy men as formators during my seminary formation and then as superiors of my community. I've had the privilege to work with countless holy men and women in Regnum Christi who have poured out their hearts for the formation of other members. Along the way, I've also met a few lemons. Not that they were necessarily bad men or women, but perhaps they were going through a trough in their own spiritual life or maybe were working through a deeper issue, or most probably my personality just brought out the worst in them.

Whatever the case, they were not successful in forming me or others under their charge, and those experiences highlighted for me four ways not to form someone. I admit these are all caricatures; that is, I haven't actually encountered individuals in the Legion of Christ or Regnum Christi who were totally like this. I've exaggerated a characteristic to highlight a negative approach that we'd do best to avoid.

I. PROJECT MANAGER

The first mistaken approach to formation comes from not understanding that we are dealing with some*one*, not some*thing*. Certain personalities—like my own—tend to see reality in function of projects to be accomplished, a mission to carry out, a job to get done… and they thrive on the sense of accomplishment that comes from checking off a box. Their very sense of self-worth can even come from what they do or how efficiently they do it.

Now, don't get me wrong. We need to get things done in the world. Good intentions and warm feelings won't milk the cows or put food on the table (as my farmer grandpa would have said). Yet, if we approach formation like just another task to accomplish or project to complete, not only will we fail in the endeavor, we can hurt people in the process. Formation is about the internal work of grace within a free human being, not a procedure carried out on a hunk of meat. While there certainly are processes involved in formation, no person can be reduced to a process.

Closely related to this impersonal approach described in this essay is the cookie cutter model. This would equate formation to external conformity to a certain ideal. There can be a deceptive comfort stemming from uniformity, as if people wearing the same clothes and following a schedule diligently were actually growing in love and Christian virtue. On the flip side, we might mistakenly think that we are free and respectful of each person's individuality by introducing non-conformity, a *laissez-faire* attitude toward scheduling and diversity of clothing styles. Both extremes are superficial and cannot be used to verify the internalization of formation or virtue. Anyone tasked with the formation of others needs to go deeper than this. External similarity can greatly contribute to the flourishing of individual personalities, as the experience of both seminaries and schools with a uniform policy has shown. On the flip side, the lack of originality in a society that professes total freedom, while most people choose the same iPhone, pick the same top clothing brands, and watch the same movies never ceases to amaze me. Real formation goes deeper than externals.

Any attitude—even in the subtlest manner—which does not acknowledge and accept the individual personality and God-given dignity of the person before me will undermine any attempts to form that person. It would be like showing up to a football game with snowshoes on. Wrong sport. Wrong equipment. Bad outcome. Don't be a formation project manager.

2. DRILL SERGEANT

During my third year in the seminary, our superior, Fr William Meade, showed us the movie *Gettysburg*. The character development of key players on that famous Pennsylvania Civil War battlefield was superbly done, drawing the audience into the personal dilemmas that each man faced. At the end of the film, a fascinating debate ensued when our superior asked us if the obedience of the Confederate officer who led his men to annihilation at Pickett's Charge was like the obedience that religious should strive to live. He knew the suicidal charge was a bad idea contrary to all military strategy, and he told General Lee so, but at the end he obeyed and led his men to death. Before the debate, I didn't really see any difference between military and religious obedience. If my superior tells me to do something, I do it, whether it makes sense or not, and whether I feel like it or not. But Fr Meade didn't agree with me. "A Legionary's obedience is never blind" he quoted us from our Constitution, explaining that obedience never requires us to act against our conscience. He then explained how Christ is the model of our obedience, and he obeyed his Father out of love.

It was an interesting lesson, but unfortunately one that I didn't learn very well right away. During my first year running Camp River Ridge in Oldenburg, Indiana, I had a group of 42 rambunctious boys and 18 counselors that were testing my patience. I was attempting to give them instructions about their next activity, but the acoustics in the gym were terrible and the poor kids had been cooped up inside for a while, so understandably they were distracted and jittery. I lost my patience and yelled out some instructions, then stormed off and left them in the hands of my head counselor. Minutes later I was surprised to watch the boys march by—literally marching—in ordered rows, calling out cadence and smiling with wide grins as they executed military maneuvers around the soccer field.

What had happened? After I left the gym, that counselor had *lowered* his voice (not raised it), gotten the boys' attention through his quiet instructions, and led them to have fun learning to march. They listened to him not because he was loud or authoritarian, but because they respected him, and he made what they were doing fun. The boys liked him, and because they did, they followed him.

I re-learned my lesson there: you cannot form someone by imposing external discipline. Formation is about internalizing attitudes and virtues, not about compliance. Authority, a loud voice, or external imposition do nothing to advance formation if respect and real love are not present.

Incidentally, that young counselor has now graduated from West Point Academy. He attributes much of his success to his formation in ECYD and Regnum Christi. I attribute more of it to his saintly mother.

3. BODYGUARD

The third caricature is the bodyguard. This is the well-intentioned person who wants to safeguard those under their care from any danger, difficulty, or even the consequences of their own mistakes. Teachers know these as helicopter or hyper-protective parents, the ones who do their child's homework for them and can't believe their little angel could ever do anything wrong.

Life is full of challenges, dangers, and evil. As a parent or someone charged with the formation of those who are not yet mature, we feel an instinctive desire to shield our charges from those dangers. There is a maternal or paternal instinct in each one of us. It is a good thing that God has placed in our hearts, but as in the case of anything good, when taken to an extreme it is vitiated. If in protecting others we do not respect them nor leave the proper space for their freedom (adapted to their age and maturity level), we fall into a paternalistic attitude. This can do more harm than good.

During the challenging months when the ugly facts about our founder's double life were beginning to seep out, I had a superior who inadvertently made that process much more painful. His motives were high and honorable: he wanted to protect me and others from the hard truth, letting it dawn on us gradually. And so instead of bringing it all out into the open at once, we got little bits and pieces over the course of a year. While his intentions were good, the effects were horrible. He couldn't control the information flow, and we were finding things out from third parties and being placed in awkward situations where outsiders knew more about the facts than we did. By trying to protect us, that superior succeeded only in undermining our trust in his honesty and good judgment.

The opposite of that paternalistic attitude is true maternal or paternal care, and it is beautiful. One of our priests remembers well his first day of school. His mom suited him up in the latest bell bottoms and plaid shirt (I don't know if that's really true, but it makes me laugh to think of him dressed like that), packed his little lunch box, and walked him to the front door. "Steve, you know the way to the school, right? You remember what your daddy showed you yesterday?" Little Steve looked out in petrified horror, nodding his head nervously. He was going to walk six blocks all by himself! Years later, he brought up the incident with his parents, recalling the terror he felt, and wondering how they could make him do that. His mother laughed, and then informed him, "You didn't see him, but your father was hiding in the bushes and followed you all the way to school that morning."

Recognizing the gifts and potential in others, pushing them out of their comfort zone, and being attentive to assist if needed: that's the spirit that should guide us. Formation doesn't come from never encountering difficulties or never failing. Formation happens when we rise from our falls, when we surmount the obstacles, and when we overcome our weakness. Paternalism just puts off those opportunities to grow.

4. POWER TRIP

The greatest and most common mistake I've witnessed over the years is unfortunately more prevalent than the preceding three. I've seen this one all too many times; I've experienced it in my own heart. It is what we can call the power trip.

A fellow priest was recently telling me about his RC women's section, where many volunteers are coming forward to offer themselves for training as spiritual guides. He related to me his concern that some were seeing this responsibility more as a feather in their cap than a service; their motives were mixed between a desire to help others and a desire to be seen as important and significant in the Movement.

There's a potent poison here. It is rarely recognized at first taste, yet if not countered, it acts relentlessly to sicken every good work undertaken for the Lord. I first noticed the symptoms of this venom in my early years of formation. Occasionally, a fellow brother would be singled out to be an auxiliary or assistant.[1] If you received this designation, certain privileges followed, like sitting at the head of the table, having others wait in deferential silence while you prayed, being able to attend a special morning snack, or participating in closed-door meetings where you were in the know about what was happening in the seminary. Some of these men's chests seemed to puff out just a bit more with all the importance of their new role. Being noticed more, being entrusted with more authority, and having their peers or subjects depend on them provided a strong temptation to make them *feel* important… and sometimes act like they actually were.

Looking back, many of those men did not persevere. Was it because God wasn't calling them? Or perhaps because the temptation to pride and an air of superiority undermined the seeds of a vocation that God had planted in them? I don't know. What I do know is that I—who was sometimes secretly envious of these chosen few— was never singled out to be a superior, but I am a priest today. It's through no merit of my own, that's for sure.

---

[1]   An auxiliary helped the assistants who were helping the novice instructor or superior. This practice and some of the perks mentioned have been curtailed in the renewal process.

Now don't get me wrong. We need structures and hierarchy and people to serve in leadership roles within the Legion and Regnum Christi. What is critical, though, is that it truly be done as a *service*, not as a power trip. As soon as the intention in a person's heart gets twisted in that direction, you can be sure that little good will come of it. Authentic formation stops where pride begins, and that holds true no matter what title you hold.

A corollary danger with this mistaken approach to formation can happen with those who subtly manipulate others by holding out to (or withholding from) them honors, perks, praise, or promises. Those to whom God has given a knack for human relations and attentiveness to the subtleties of the human psyche can misuse this gift by learning just which buttons to push to get people to do what they want. Any use of this gift that does not respect the dignity and freedom of another person is an abuse.

During our period of renewal, I have seen so much good fruit come from a refreshed look at the service of authority. The observance of term limits, consultations for roles within the Movement, and openness to people outside the prior parameters to serve in roles of authority have all been bearing good fruit. The Holy See's document on this topic, "The Service of Authority and Obedience"[2] presents an excellent antidote to the poison of pride in the exercise of authority. Positions within the Legion and the Movement should never give the impression of a caste system or of a power trip for the guys calling the shots. If you are called to serve others, it is as Christ taught us:

---

2   Congregation for Institutes of Consecrated Life and Societies of Apostolic Life, May 11, 2008. This document can be found online.

Jesus summoned them and said, "You know that the rulers of the Gentiles lord it over them, and the great ones make their authority over them felt. But it shall not be so among you. Rather, whoever wishes to be great among you shall be your servant; whoever wishes to be first among you shall be your slave. Just so, the Son of Man did not come to be served but to serve and to give his life as a ransom for many."

—Matthew 20:25–28

2. HOW JESUS FORMED HIS APOSTLES

I had a shop teacher in high school who was missing the tips of three fingers. He gave us an explanation one day of how to use the radial arm saw. He began by holding up his hand. "This is what can happen if you think you know what you are doing with this saw." Needless to say, he caught our attention, and we took careful note of how to pull the arm, where to place our hands, and what safeguards to take.

I hope the four ways *not* to form someone have caught your attention because formation in the Movement is a serious matter; the fulfillment of our mission depends on it. Let us now attempt to answer the question *how* by turning to the model of our Christian life, Jesus Christ. From him, the Master and model, we learn how to contribute to the formation of others. When we examine the Gospels, we find four ways that Jesus went about forming his apostles.

1. JESUS CALLED THEM AND INVITED THEM INTO HIS LIFE

Now, in my human way of seeing things, if I were going to start the Church in Jesus' time, I wouldn't have started where Jesus did. And I wouldn't have chosen whom he did. If you want a culture transforming movement, you go to the epicenter of culture. Rome was where it was at: the empire, the power, the intellectuals, and the money were all there. And if you want to change things, you go to the leaders: the chief priest, King Herod, the governor, and the emperor.

Yet, God's ways are not man's ways. The three wise men did not find Jesus in the king's palace nor in the splendor of imperial Rome, but in a podunk village on the fringes of the Roman Empire. Jesus did not choose the chief priests and scribes and religious leaders of his day to start his Church. He did not even select particularly capable individuals. As we read in Mark 3:13–15:

> He went up the mountain and summoned those whom he wanted and they came to him. He appointed twelve (whom he also named apostles) that they might be with him and he might send them forth to preach and to have authority to drive out demons.

Yes, years later, Peter and Paul would bring the Church to the heart of the Roman Empire; nobles, kings, and emperors would all eventually pay homage to the Lord of time and history. But that is not where Jesus began. Throughout salvation history, we find this same puzzling paradox played out. Saints from remote villages evangelized the great cities. Ignorant peasants rose to become the greatest saints. Notorious sinners repented and became examples of purity and piety. St. Paul put his finger on it when he wrote:

> Rather, God chose the foolish of the world to shame the wise, and God chose the weak of the world to shame the strong, and God chose the lowly and despised of the world, those who count for nothing, to reduce to nothing those who are something, so that no human being might boast before God.
>
> —1 Corinthians 1:27–29

It is as if God wanted to prove that there is always hope, and that he can make something out of nothing. Jesus began with twelve simple men having no outstanding experience, knowledge, connections, or qualifications. What was special is that he called them. His very selection of them raised them up and set them apart.

What happened next was of even greater importance. Not only did Jesus choose them, but he shared his life with them. This wasn't a comic book movie, where the protagonist is bitten by a spider and suddenly has super powers that he uses to save the world from cataclysmic fiends. No, to prepare the apostles for their mission, Jesus patiently spent three long years with them. They lived together. They chatted around a campfire, went on long walks from one town to another, and spent time fishing. Jesus preached and they listened along with the crowds, but then he explained more to them in private. They got front-row seats to witness miracles, beheld the delight in the eyes of the blind man as he saw for the first time, and unwrapped the bandages from Lazarus who emerged from the tomb.

At the core of all this is one simple fact: Jesus spent time with his apostles. That was the first way that Jesus formed them.

2. JESUS MODELED LOVE FOR THEM

We are so familiar with some Gospel passages that our eyes glaze over when we hear more words like, "Whatever you did for one of these least brothers of mine, you did for me." That's why words will never be enough; the world needs witnesses, people who practice what they preach.

A few years ago, two Legionary brothers were walking back from St. Peter's Basilica in Rome. Half a block ahead they saw—or perhaps smelled first—a homeless man panhandling on the street corner. His long and shaggy beard mixed with unkempt hair poking out from under a gray stocking cap, and grubby fingers stretched out begging for alms from the passersby. Brother Jason caught one whiff of the putrid odor of unwashed flesh, liquor, and vomit and quickly crossed over to the other side of the street as if to escape. Brother Cliff walked straight up to the poor man, knelt down before him, took his gnarled hands in his own, and then looked into his eyes and asked him his name. Today, Fr. Jason Smith often remembers that lesson as he meets Jesus in the guise of homeless people in Manhattan, taking time to ask them their name and pray with them. The lesson that Fr. Cliff Ermatinger taught him did not contain a single word, yet will never be forgotten.

This is what Jesus did with his apostles. He *modeled* for them the attitudes, actions, and kind of life that he wanted his followers to live. When you spend as much time as the apostles did with Jesus, you pick up on a lot of things. They learned what made him tick, his deepest motivations, what could stir him to sudden anger, and what made his eyes light up with joy. The apostles learned so much from Jesus by this daily observation.

Reading the Gospel narratives, we also get a clear sense that Jesus was quite intentional in his interactions with the apostles. He knew that he was preparing them for a mission, as is evident from the first moment of their calling. "Come after me, and I will make you fishers of men." (Mk 1:17) They were not out for a pleasure jaunt, but because Jesus wanted to involve them in the greatest adventure of human history, the most noble and heroic of all missions: the salvation of souls.

This is particularly evident in the first chapter of Mark's Gospel. As the apostles walked with Jesus, he displayed his divine authority (cf. Mk 1:22, 1:27), proved his power over bodily ailments and spiritual sickness (cf. Mk 1:34), attested to the source of that power through his union with the Father in prayer (cf. Mk 1:35), and alluded to the universality of his mission (cf. Mk 1:38–39). He revealed to them why he had come: to preach, to fulfill the law and promises, to heal, to save (cf. Mk 1:38, 1:44, 2:11). And perhaps most importantly, Jesus revealed to his apostles his own heart. The pity, mercy, and love that exuded from each of his actions and decisions became so apparent that decades later the apostle John would capture the essence of Jesus' very being in the simple phrase: "God is love." He then explained:

> God is love. In this way the love of God was revealed to us: God sent his only Son into the world so that we might have life through him. In this is love: not that we have loved God, but that he loved us and

sent his Son as expiation for our sins. Beloved, if God so loved us, we also must love one another. No one has ever seen God. Yet, if we love one another, God remains in us, and his love is brought to perfection in us.

—I John 4:8–12

I think that sometimes we can be a bit naïve about the radical nature of Christ's life and message. We look at things from the standpoint of a Christian worldview, after two millennia of Gospel criteria being lived out and enculturated into our ways of doing things. But for the apostles, living in a pre-Christian world—where brutal beatings of fellow humans, callous treatment of women, discarding of diseased persons, usury, slavery, and prostitution were everyday occurrences—Christ's radical concern for each individual person stood out.

And Jesus did not merely *teach* his apostles; he *modeled* this charity for them. Day in and day out, they saw his tenderness of heart with children (cf. Lk 18:16), his anger at obstinacy or flippancy with his Father's house (cf. Mt 15:14, 21:12), his pity for the widow's loss (cf. Lk 7:13), his attentiveness to the widow's gift (cf. Mk 12:43–44), and his inability to say no to anyone who was in need (cf. Mt 15:28, 20:26–34; Mk 10:46–52; Lk 17:12–14). His every action bled out the charity in his heart. And when his heart was physically bleeding out on the Cross, even then he taught and modeled—for them and for us today—saying with his dying breath, "Father, forgive them." (Lk 23:34)

Observations can lead to internal soul-searching, to a change of heart, to the molding of a new heart. The apostles observed all these things day after day for three years. Jesus' actions spoke louder than his words. His witness of life and love was one of the most powerful ways that he formed his apostles.

3. JESUS CORRECTED THEM[3]

One of the greatest lies of our time is that it is rude, inconsiderate, and un-Christian to correct someone. Swept along by the relativism of our time, even many Catholics balk at the idea of fraternal correction. For some, it is a mistaken reading of our Lord's injunction, "Stop judging, that you may not be judged." (Mt 7:1) For others, it is a mistaken idea of charity, as if any conflict were to be avoided. Such interpretations do not jive with Scripture or Christian tradition.[4]

This becomes crystal clear with a few examples. If your friend is about to reach out and touch an electrified fence, you might not be friends anymore if you neglect to cry out a warning. If a doctor decides not to warn a patient about the gravity of his condition because he doesn't want to make him feel bad, he risks losing his medical license. A traffic cop who just waves and grins at cars as they go by might make us smile, but he'll have a hard time explaining to his commanding officer why there were three accidents on his watch. There are times

---

3   In this section, I have purposely left out references to Jesus' corrections of the Pharisees, merchants in the Temple, and other groups. Some of the most resounding corrections in the Gospels are for them, but here I am focusing on what Jesus does to form his followers.

4   Cf. John 7:24 "Stop judging by appearances, but judge justly." Many other passages throughout the Old and New Testaments attest to the importance of proper judgment, admonishment of sinners, and fraternal correction (cf. 2 Sam 7:14; Sir 19: 12–16; Mt 7:2; Rom 2:1–3, 15:14; Gal 6:1; Col 3:16; 1 Thes 5:12–14; Titus 1:13, 2:15). The Catholic Church's tradition captures this in one of the seven spiritual works of mercy: admonish the sinner. I highly recommend Edward Sri's excellent book on this topic, "Who Am I to Judge?"

and situations in which not acting, not judging, or not correcting are a gross negligence of duty or a lack of charity. A certain amount of good education and timing is undoubtedly necessary, but correction of some type will always be needed if we really do care about someone.

In the case of our Lord, correction and admonishment were instrumental in forming his apostles for the mission. His driving motive for correcting was always love for the person. Not exasperation, impatience, irritation, annoyance… but love. He had a knack for adopting the right tone, choosing the right moment, and using the force necessary for each person.

• *Quiet and pained*

Jesus used quiet and indirect rebukes—practically entreaties of the heart for repentance—when he saw that someone's mind was set on evil. We can hear the tender pain in Jesus' voice at the Last Supper when he turns to Peter and says:

"Simon, Simon, behold Satan has demanded to sift all of you like wheat, but I have prayed that your own faith may not fail; and once you have turned back, you must strengthen your brothers." He said to him, "Lord, I am prepared to go to prison and to die with you." But he replied, "I tell you, Peter, before the cock crows this day, you will deny three times that you know me."

—Lk 22:31–34

As Jesus washed the feet of Judas, we can only imagine the expressions that crossed his visage, knowing full well what the traitor would do. "What you are going to do, do quickly." (Jn 13:27) It is quiet reproach, resigned, yet still hopeful of conversion. And a short time later in the garden, Judas "went up to Jesus to kiss him. Jesus said to him, 'Judas, are you betraying the Son of Man with a kiss?'" (Lk 22:47–48)

• *Gentle chiding*

There were many moments of gentle chiding. Jesus called to Peter on his boat after the miraculous catch of fish, and Peter cried out, "Depart from me, Lord, for I am a sinful man." But Jesus reassured him, saying "Do not be afraid; from now on you will be catching men." (Lk 5:8–10) Jesus also gently scolds the apostles for sleeping in his hour of need (cf. Lk 22:46).

At the last supper, Philip said to Jesus, "Master, show us the Father, and that will be enough for us." Jesus replied to him:

> Have I been with you for so long a time and you still do not know me, Philip? Whoever has seen me has seen the Father. How can you say, "Show us the Father"? Do you not believe that I am in the Father and the Father is in me?
>
> —Jn 14:8–10

After the resurrection, Jesus had to correct Mary Magdalene and tell her, "Stop holding on to me, for I have not yet ascended to the Father." All these corrections from our Lord came when the person in question, insecure or misguided in love, needed a gentle nudge. There is no ill will, and a light hint is all that is needed to reorient.

- *Group corrections of attitude or criteria*

When an important lesson needed to be conveyed or an attitude set straight, Jesus wasn't afraid to conduct group chewing-out sessions. When children were being brought to Jesus and the disciples rebuked them, Jesus immediately and publicly corrected them, "Let the children come to me, and do not prevent them; for the kingdom of heaven belongs to such as these." (Mt 19:13–14)

On another occasion, in Luke 22:24–26, "an argument broke out among them about which of them should be regarded as the greatest." Here was a key moment to set them straight and help them see the type of leadership he expected of his followers. "He said to them, 'The kings of the Gentiles lord it over them and those in authority over them are addressed as "Benefactors"; but among you it shall not be so.'" Jesus sets a higher standard for those in his Kingdom who would lead, or for those who would attempt to contribute to the formation of others. "Rather, let the greatest among you be as the youngest, and the leader as the servant." This was a crucial lesson, so important that each of the Gospel narratives includes a similar message (cf. Mt 23:11, Mk 9:34–37, Jn 13:13–15). Jesus doesn't want us to miss this lesson.

- *Bolstering their faith*

On various occasions, Jesus upbraided his disciples for their lack of faith or slowness to grasp what was important. When he warned them to be on guard against the leaven of the Pharisees and of Herod (cf. Mk 8:13–21), the apostles got the wrong message and Jesus had to clarify:

"Do you not yet understand or comprehend? Are your hearts hardened? Do you have eyes and not see, ears and not hear? And do you not remember, when I broke the five loaves for the five thousand, how many wicker baskets full of fragments you picked up?" They answered him, "Twelve." "When I broke the seven loaves for the four thousand, how many full baskets of fragments did you pick up?" They answered (him), "Seven." He said to them, "Do you still not understand?"

When Jesus arrived at the tomb of Lazarus, he gave them a direct command, "'Take away the stone.' Martha, the dead man's sister, said to him, 'Lord, by now there will be a stench; he has been dead for four days.' Jesus said to her, 'Did I not tell you that if you believe you will see the glory of God?'" (Jn 11:39–40) We can imagine the tender look on Jesus' face as he consoles Martha and strengthens her faith.

When the faith of the disciples was too insecure to cast out the demon from a possessed boy, and the boy's father said, "I brought him to your disciples, but they could not cure him," Jesus said in reply, "O faithless and perverse generation, how long will I be with you? How long will I endure you? Bring him here to me." (Mt 17:16–17) Jesus was reproving his disciples for their lack of faith.

• *Direct and forceful*

Jesus also corrected individuals directly and forcefully, particularly Peter. Immediately after Jesus had told him he would be the rock on which he would build his Church, Peter seemed to go on a power trip and thought he could now give some advice to Jesus about avoiding suffering. Jesus "turned to him and said, 'Get behind me, Satan! You are an obstacle to me. You are thinking not as God does, but as human beings do.'" (Mt 16:23) In the garden of Gethsemane, Peter's impulsive nature leads him to strike out with his sword to cut off Malchus' right ear, and Jesus reprimands him, "Put your sword into its scabbard. Shall I not drink the cup that the Father gave me?" (Jn 18:10–11). Similar corrections are found in Luke 22:38 and 23:49–51.

Correction was a crucial tool for Jesus to form his disciples. They remembered the lessons so well that they are recorded throughout the Gospels, with no shame. We see clearly that Jesus corrected his apostles because he loved them, because he wanted to prepare them for the mission he was entrusting to them.

4. JESUS SENT THEM ON A MISSION

This mission that Jesus would entrust to them, of making disciples of all nations, was so far beyond their capacities and horizons of possibility that if they had known it from the first, they probably would have walked away saying, "This is hard; who can accept it?" (Jn 6:60). Perhaps that is why Jesus *didn't* entrust the mission from the first moment; he called, he shared his life with them, revealed to them the love in his heart, and then gave them a little taste of success.

Jesus formed his followers well. Before the big game, he ran basic drills, then had them gain confidence with scrimmages. The first chapters of the Gospels are replete with Jesus giving instruction to his disciples and letting them witness his miracles. Then, they got the nod to get into the game. In Matthew 10:5–10 we read that:

⌐Jesus sent out these twelve after instructing them thus, "Do not go into pagan territory or enter a Samaritan town. Go rather to the lost sheep of the house of Israel. As you go, make this proclamation: 'The kingdom of heaven is at hand.' Cure the sick, raise the dead, cleanse lepers, drive out demons. Without cost you have received; without cost you are to give. Do not take gold or silver or copper for your belts; no sack for the journey, or a second tunic, or sandals, or walking stick. The laborer deserves his keep."

This first mission trip gave them a taste of the bigger mission that awaits them. Luke 10:1–11 relates a similar mission trip. He gave them clear instructions; he set clear parameters to the work at hand; he sent them out; and then he was there to welcome them back and have a mission debriefing (cf. Lk 10:17–24).

The passion and death of our Lord shook up the apostles. Peter—first among the apostles—denied him and the others fled. Even after the Resurrection, they remained fearfully locked in the upper room. The experience of suffering in our lives tends to move us to do the same. Yet human life cannot be understood without reconciling the reality of suffering with the reality of the resurrection, and that is why the apostles were not sent out on their mission until "he opened their minds to understand the scriptures" (Lk 24:45) and they were "clothed with power from on high." (Lk 24:49)

Through the power of the Holy Spirit—not by their own power—they were ready to take on the mission.

> Then Jesus approached and said to them, "All power in heaven and on earth has been given to me. Go, therefore, and make disciples of all nations, baptizing them in the name of the Father, and of the Son, and of the holy Spirit, teaching them to observe all that I have commanded you. And behold, I am with you always, until the end of the age."
>
> —Mt 28:18–20

5. SUMMING UP: LOVE LIKE CHRIST, FORM LIKE CHRIST

These four ways that Jesus formed his apostles are beautifully reflected in my favorite number of the Legion's Constitution, n. 4.

> In their mission of forming apostles, Christian leaders at the service of the Church, Legionaries make present the mystery of Christ gathering the Apostles around him, revealing to them the love of his heart, forming them, and sending them out to collaborate with him in building up his Kingdom.

Each member of the Regnum Christi Movement lives this according to his or her own state in life, in accordance with age, sex, unique gifts, and life experience. What unites us all is what one young woman from the Philippines said when summing up our charism: "We seek to love so much that it creates in others a desire to love like that in return." That's the formation that Christ imparted to his apostles.

3. IMPLICATIONS FOR REGNUM CHRISTI

The fourfold approach that Jesus took in forming his apostles—choosing, modeling, correcting, and sending—has three immediate implications that I see for Regnum Christi. I'm sure that you will form your own personal conclusions as well.

I. APPROACH TO FORMATION

Is the emphasis on a certain role for RC members who form others—call it what you may—something particular to Regnum Christi?

I think we'd be a bit naïve to think so. There are many other groups within the Church that recognize the need to form lay people. The Vincentians have even gone so far as to speak of them as "formators" analogously, as we have. In reality, neither the term nor the concept is exclusive to Regnum Christi. Alongside many others in the Church, we assign a special importance to this role, though I also think we have a special knack for forming lay people according to our Christ-centered spirituality.

In Regnum Christi, we are called to form apostles as Christ himself did. That does not mean "formation" in the abstract, as if it were some sort of assembly line production process. Our style of formation should avoid the four pitfalls mentioned in this essay and exemplify the style that Christ himself adopted. That means, first of all, that authentic formation cannot begin without a deep experience of the love of Jesus Christ and his personal call. Pope Francis captured this beautifully in his Easter Vigil homily in 2014:

In the life of every Christian, after baptism there is also a more existential "Galilee": the experience of a personal encounter with Jesus Christ who called me to follow him and to share in his mission. In this sense, returning to Galilee means treasuring in my heart the living memory of that call, when Jesus passed my way, gazed at me with mercy, and asked me to follow him. It means reviving the memory of that moment when his eyes met mine, the moment when he made me realize that he loved me.[5]

If we are entrusted with the formation of another person—whether it be your son or daughter, a student, or a fellow member of Regnum Christi—your first task is to help them experience or revive that profound encounter with Christ. Without that, nothing else matters.

Once that starting point is there, then we can continue the formation process loving as Christ did, teaching and reproving rooted in respect for the dignity and freedom of the person, and always with the end goal in sight.

What is clear from the Gospels is that Christ formed his apostles in a personal, hands-on, experiential way. In the past few years, we have been discovering that the younger generations require just this approach. We are already applying this in ECYD, which is the way that Regnum Christi brings its charism into working with youth. The very name implies this method: Encounters with (or Experiences of) Jesus Christ that lead to deeply held [i.e. Your] Convictions, that result in Decisions to live as a Christian. ECYD is the future of Regnum Christi, and every member should be concerned for its growth and development.

---

5   POPE FRANCIS, Easter Vigil Homily, April 19, 2014.

2. RECRUITMENT AND PACE OF GROWTH

A second conclusion we can draw from these reflections is that recruitment of new members to Regnum Christi should never be a contest to see who has the most personal influence over others, a manipulation of people to make them part of my cause, or a numbers game. As our young lady from the Philippines stated so aptly, "We seek to love so much that it creates in others a desire to love like that in return."

When we find someone who wants to love as Jesus does, who identifies with our spirituality and Christian way of life, and who feels at home within our spiritual family in the Catholic Church, then it is natural and good to invite them to join Regnum Christi.

Over the years, I have asked a simple question in many different localities: "How did Regnum Christi grow here?" Initially, I was very surprised by the responses. I was expecting people to have joined because of some important apostolate that was impacting culture or due to a great recruitment pipeline. Invariably, the answer was much simpler. "I joined because [X person] invited me. I respected them." Other contributing factors may have helped in the process, but the key was almost always the personal invitation of a respected peer. I found another surprise in the responses: in almost every locality, just a handful of Regnum Christi members did most of the inviting.

What does this tell us about the future of Regnum Christi growth? This experience seems to imply that the Movement will never grow exponentially. It will be organic, person by person. To the extent that we have members who love like Christ and become great mentors for others, in that measure Regnum Christi will grow.

In the history of the Church, many great groups—some that even shared a spirit and dynamism similar to ours in their first years—have died out.[6] Why? I think it is because of two main factors that are interrelated: (1) they became happy with their groups of friends and (2) they failed to attract new members. As the years went by, the movement became a sociological grouping rather than dynamic, Christ-centered teams. They were fine together and may have even been growing in their formation, but they stopped attracting new people. They also stopped attracting younger people, who are always drawn to love, exuberance, and a lofty ideal. Hence, the importance of Regnum Christi's youth work—i.e. ECYD—for the future.

How can we avoid this same death spiral?[7] The only way is to stay rooted in Christ, being forever rejuvenated in his love. That is the secret to evangelization, to growth, and to relevance. We should imitate Christ's appreciation for youth and his readiness to take the risk of letting young people lead. Older members should recognize their mission to form the younger generation, then relinquish positions and let them lead, remaining as mentors. May our Lord grant that Regnum Christi continue to attract those who want to form themselves for the mission and not merely become complacent with a closed circle of pious friends.

---

6   Many groups are listed at https://en.wikipedia.org/wiki/List_of_defunct_ Catholic_religious_institutes. A review of the Annuario Pontificio gives statistics on the decline of many other groups that are nearing extinction.

7   I make an unspoken assumption here. Namely, that God wants us to continue to exist and grow. In theory, it is possible that God would raise up a new order or movement, but not intend it to continue until the end of history. Many groups in the Church have indeed died out, and that would be fascinating material for an academic study on the causes of decline and to what degree it was linked to the members' own sinful neglect or to changes in historical circumstances that no longer required that charism in the life of the Church.

3. WHAT DO WE CALL THOSE WHO CARRY OUT REGNUM CHRISTI'S APPROACH TO FORMATION?

During my first years in the Legion, I worked with a significant number of people from many countries. I began to read sources of our spirituality in Spanish, while also studying Latin and Greek. We would joke sometimes among the seminarians about our bumbling mistakes in speaking one language or another. Due to our extensive mixing up of languages, Fr. Owen Kearns and Fr. Anthony Bannon compiled a "Style Guide" to correct some of the more egregious butcherings of English. We gradually eliminated "Spanglish" terms from our vocabulary, terms such as "aclaration" (clarification), "captation" (recruitment), "cavilate" (speculate), "collaborator" (co-worker or volunteer), "consecrated ladies" (consecrated women), "fervorous" (fervent), "put attention" (pay attention), and "sympathizer" (supporter).

It was only later, when I began my internship and then priestly ministry, that I realized the importance of this precision in language. At times when I would lapse into a foreign term or use a specialized word, I would get blank looks or puzzled faces. Those one or two words could become obstacles to transmitting the Gospel, either because people thought I was too big for my britches with those fancy terms, or because they got hung up on the words and lost the bigger message. So gradually I've become a firm believer in using words well, translating English as English (and not Spanglish or Latinized English), and avoiding jargon.

When I contributed to the translation of documents such as *"The Formation of RC Formators"* and the *RC Member Handbook* years ago, we looked for an English term as a translation for the rich Spanish word "formador". In those translations from Spanish, we settled on "formator," and in many of our Regnum Christi circles this has become a common term that conveys much of what I have described in this essay.

Over the past several years, though, I have begun to notice the blank looks on new members' faces whenever I used the term. Bishops or priests would think I was talking about seminary life if I used the term "formator". Then, when Microsoft Word kept underlining it with a squiggly red line, I investigated a bit further. I encountered three issues with the word that just won't go away.

1. Used commonly in the Church's documents?

The word "formator" does appear repeatedly throughout official translations into English of Catholic Church documents. However, the vast majority of those citations are referring specifically to seminary formators, and *not* to those engaged in the formation of lay people in general. The accepted usage of it within the broader Catholic Church is only for seminaries and formation houses of religious and consecrated.

2. Not a word in common English usage.

I have been able to find one or two rare occasions in translations of Pope Francis' more recent discourses into English where the term "formator" is used with broader reference than just seminary formators. This makes sense when we realize that Pope Francis is a native Spanish speaker, and the term "formador" in Spanish is commonly accepted in everyday language. A quick Google search turns up the definition in Spanish, "a person who dedicates themselves to educate others." That's beautiful, and conveys the concepts described in this essay; that is why the term was adopted in the Movement's Spanish language materials.

When it comes to English, though, a search for the term "formator" on Google turns up the following:

*Noun. (plural formators) (semiotics) A symbol that indicates a relationship between designators.

What does this mean? Well, unless you are planning to use the term for specialized semiotics, you probably shouldn't be using it in English. There is no other definition listed. Most dictionaries won't even have *that* listing, let alone a definition comparable to the Spanish one. Why? Because it is not a word in the English language, except in the specialized semiotic (science) or seminary (Catholic) domain.

3. Language is always evolving. Could "formator" be a neologism?

Yes, language is continually evolving. Yet the usage of any new term must be widespread throughout culture, otherwise it will simply be jargon, i.e. language only understood by a few people within a closed group. While jargon may contribute to a group's members feeling close-knit and special because they understand each other, it will simultaneously separate them from outsiders. Regnum Christi has a mission to evangelize the culture, not merely remain a cliquish group worried about its own formation. If our specialized vocabulary alienates people, inadvertently makes them feel like they don't know what we are talking about, or impedes our ability to transmit the Gospel message to the people outside our circle… well, then I think we have a serious problem. Regnum Christi is called to form apostles who can transmit the Gospel, not simply spin stories to the choir. For the foreseeable future, there is no chance of "formator" becoming vernacular in the culture. It's not going to be a neologism; it already is jargon.

So, what should we call those who form others? The rich concept we want to convey should not be lost. It is a big part of what we do in Regnum Christi. After all, we are all about forming apostles, and *someone* has to contribute to that formation.

Now, if there were no adequate word in English, I'd agree that we need to invent one, and perhaps "formator" would be the most adequate. In my search, however, for alternate translations for the Spanish "formador", I came across several options, including apostle, guide, and supporter, but the most interesting one seems to be *mentor*.

Now, we all know the common English word "mentor." What people often don't know is the story behind it. A Google search on the word "mentor" turns up the following:

> Mentor (mĕn'tər, –tôr), in Greek mythology, friend of Odysseus and tutor of Telemachus. On several occasions in the Odyssey, Athena assumes Mentor's form to give advice to Telemachus or Odysseus. His name is proverbial for a faithful and wise adviser.

There's a lot to unpack in that short definition. There's a story there, and I love stories. If you've never read the epic adventure of the Odyssey, you've missed out on one of the most important works in world literature. The hero

Odysseus sets out to battle with his Greek companions for the fated city of Troy. He must leave behind the wife he loves and his young son Telemachus, but he places them in the trusted hands of Mentor. This marvelous man does more than his duty' he protects Odysseus' wife Penelope from suitors who claim her husband is dead, he loves Telemachus as his own son, and he guides the young man to find his father. There are even moments when a goddess speaks in his guise to provide wise counsel to the key characters. Mentor is more than a term or an idea; he was a person, a friend, an adviser, a tutor, and a voice for the divine. Mentor did not mold or form an inanimate object, but trained up a boy in freedom, accompanying him on his growth in virtue and progress into manhood.

As I researched the term, I found that it is widely used and has a nearly universally positive connotation in the English-speaking world. As Wikipedia states, "the personal name Mentor has been adopted in English as a term meaning someone who imparts wisdom to and shares knowledge with a less experienced colleague." It seems to me to capture quite well the concept that we seek to live out in Regnum Christi: to accompany a person that we love along the paths of God to their fulfillment in Christ. "My children, for whom I am again in labor until Christ be formed in you!" (Gal 4:19)

I love the richness contained in the word, and if I had my druthers, I'd replace all usage of the jargon term "formator" from Regnum Christi circles with "mentor."

CONCLUSION

Regardless of what happens with our terminology, I have great confidence in the future of Regnum Christi. We are not perfect and never will be, yet we have already been recognized for the excellent formation of our members. The caliber of our people, the enhanced clarity of our charism after this period of renewal, and the increased enthusiasm I find in members across the North American Territory and worldwide all bode well for the years to come. We have much to be grateful for and much to look forward to.

My deepest prayer is that we truly do live Christ-centered lives, being rejuvenated each day in his love. Apostolic dynamism will flow naturally from that love. May our formation in Regnum Christi—illuminated by the answer to the question "*how* do we form?" in this essay—continue to bear great fruit for our mission of forming the apostles the Church and the world so desperately need today.

—Fr Daniel Brandenburg, LC

APPENDIX

DISCUSSION QUESTIONS (FOR A GROUP)

1. Who were the one or two teachers, coaches, or mentors who most impacted my life? What traits did I most admire in them?

2. Who in the Movement helped me most to encounter Christ? Who inspired me to join Regnum Christi?

3. How do we practice Christian fraternal correction in a world that twists Christ's words "do not judge" into an unrecognizable and un-Christian attitude of relativism?

4. How can we apply the Movement's principle of "do, get, let" to launch new apostles? (cf. RC Member Handbook #352)

5. What can our section or locality do to ensure that we are constantly rejuvenating?

6. What term do you think we should use to denote those in Regnum Christi who fulfill some role in formation?

PRACTICAL EXAM (FOR PERSONAL USE)

1. What grade would I give myself in each of the four steps of how Jesus formed?

    o   Called   _____
    o   Model   _____
    o   Correct   _____
    o   Launch   _____

2. Do I practice fraternal correction in a Christian way?

3. Do I practice the Movement's principle of "do, get, let" to launch new apostles? (cf. RC Member Handbook #352)

4. What attitudes, skills, or behaviors do I need to develop to form others like Christ did?

5. What am I going to continue doing?

6. What am I going to modify in myself, with God's grace? What will I foster in those I work with?

7. Does it feel natural to me to invite someone to join Regnum Christi? If not, what holds me back?

EXPLORING MORE

Please visit our website, *RCSpirituality.org* for more spiritual resources, and follow us on Facebook for regular updates: *facebook.com/RCSpirituality*

Study Circle Guides are a service of Regnum Christi and the Legionaries of Christ.
RegnumChristi.org & *LegionofChrist.org*

Produced by Coronation.
CoronationMedia.com

Developed & Self-published by RCSpirituality.

Made in the USA
Columbia, SC
23 February 2018